Sculptured bedrock covered with lichen, Lake Superior shoreline at Grand Marais

TEXT BY DOUGLAS WOOD
PHOTOGRAPHY BY GREG RYAN

MINNESOTA

THE SPIRIT
OF THE LAND

VOYAGEUR PRESS

Edited by Michael Dregni
Designed by Kathryn Mallien
Printed in Hong Kong
95 96 97 98 99 5 4 3 2 1

Library of Congress Cataloging-in-Publication Data
    Wood, Douglas, 1951–
        Minnesota, the spirit of the land / text by Douglas Wood ; photography
    by Greg Ryan.
            p.   cm.
        ISBN 0-89658-310-4
        1. Minnesota—Pictorial works. 2. Minnesota—Description and travel. I. Title.
    F607.W66   1995
    977.6—dc20   95-4107
                                                                                   CIP

Published by Voyageur Press, Inc.
P.O. Box 338, 123 North Second Street, Stillwater, MN 55082 USA
612-430-2210   •   fax 612-430-2211

Please write or call, or stop by, for our free catalog of natural history publications.
Our toll-free number to place an order or to obtain a free catalog is 800-888-WOLF
(800-888-9653).

Educators, fundraisers, premium and gift buyers, publicists, and marketing managers:
Looking for creative products and new sales ideas? Voyageur Press books are available
at special discounts when purchased in quantities, and special editions can be created
to your specifications. For details contact our marketing department.

Pages 2–3: Fall colors surround the Onion River in the Superior National Forest

Rapids on the Kawishiwi River in the Boundary Waters Canoe Area, Superior National Forest

DEDICATIONS

To Sally Beyer, my partner and friend, whose dedication, determination, skill,
and support made this project possible. — *GR*

To Mary E. Wood, who epitomized the enduring, generous beauty of this land. — *DW*

ACKNOWLEDGMENTS

My sincere appreciation to Michael Dregni for suggestions and insight in editing this manuscript; to Kathy Mallien for her artistic perception and hard work in weaving together the words and images; and to Tom Lebovsky and the entire staff at Voyageur Press for their enthusiastic assistance in the planning and preparation of this book. Thanks to Sally Beyer for seeing the possibilities early on and helping bring the whole project to fruition. Special thanks go to my wife, Kathy, for typing and criticism, constant encouragement and faith. And, of course, my deepest gratitude to Greg Ryan for the superb images that bring the book to life. — *DW*

CONTENTS

Wild cherry, aspen, birch, and spruce in fall, Split Rock
Lighthouse State Park

INTRODUCTION

Red pine at dawn in the Boundary Waters Canoe Area Wilderness

Dawn over Minnesota, and on some North Woods point a ragged red pine stands tattooed against a crimson sky. To the east, Lake Superior still slumbers, breathing softly beneath the battlements of Palisade Head and Split Rock, while to the west, the infant Mississippi creeps near hushed corridors of old-growth pine, then wanders through the heartland toward union with the St. Croix.

Together the great waters swing south and east, rolling through a land of limestone bluffs, trout-stream valleys, and hardwood forests—"driftless" country that never knew the grip of the Wisconsin glaciation. While farther west, the prairie greets the dawn as it always has, a stream-side cottonwood shivering in the first breeze, quartzite cliffs turning from black to burgundy, a red-tailed hawk screaming a challenge to the sun.

This is Minnesota as it has been for ten millennia, since the retreat of the last ice sheets. And although now at the dawn of the twenty-first century the imprint of humanity is never hard to find, still these things abide. The rivers still roll to the sea, singing the songs of the unremembered ages. The cliffs still catch the first hues of morning, the pines still reach for the sky. The prairie hills still roll toward far western horizons. The North Woods lakes still shrug off their morning blanket of fog and echo with the call of the loon.

Summer, Upper Red Lake

Such scenes offer, as they always have, solace and perspective and inspiration, as well as a mirrored glimpse into the landscape within. For the geography of the land is also the geography of the soul. Every hill climbed is climbed in the mind as well. Every crossing of lake or river is also a traverse of the heart. As Longfellow wrote, "All things are symbols. The external shows of nature have their image in the mind."

So it is that forests and glades and solitary shores and burnished hills are reflected within. Such things are part of the ancient memory of the species. They are the language of dreams and visions and an unquenchable longing etched deep within our collective subconscious. The poets tell us this, as do the great spiritual texts of the world.

And so in Minnesota these natural things endure—places of beauty and mystery, sanctuaries of the spirit, hiding places of "the real." And they speak, in whispers or in siren songs, to those who seek them out—or who find them by accident while searching, it was thought, for something else.

I have been in love with Minnesota for a long time. My family's roots run deep, dating back to farmers and homesteaders Colonel James George and Caleb Emery in 1852, through my Aunt Mary, who lived all her life in the area of Rochester, Douglas, and Oronoco, and my father who grew up there, too. But it was as a visitor, not as a resident, that I first fell in love with the state, journeying one summer at age seven from Iowa, where my dad was a teacher, to the Great North Woods. I returned to Iowa that fall, but my heart never did. I had found my "favorite place on Earth," and that has never changed.

As I grew older, I promised myself that someday I would move to Minnesota, and eventually I did, teaching school for a time on the western prairies; exploring the north country as a wilderness guide and naturalist; rediscovering my family's roots in the southeast.

Eventually my own family settled in central Minnesota, on a pine-clad bend in the Mississippi. My work as a naturalist and performer often called for me to crisscross the state, and along the way I

Silver maple leaves in Mississippi bottomlands

explored as many wild, lovely, and out-of-the-way places as I could find. I still do.

Through it all, that childhood love affair with Minnesota has grown and deepened to the point where I can imagine living nowhere else.

My feelings and recollections are best recorded in words. Greg Ryan finds his expression through photographs. His haunting images on these pages present wild Minnesota at its best, and portray some of the scenes I love the most. I'm grateful to Greg for his invitation to write the text to accompany the spectacular pictures.

It is with deep pleasure, and with the feeling of fulfilling an old but once vague dream, that I join Greg Ryan in presenting these visions of the spirit of the land that is Minnesota.

NORTH WOODS

Red- and white-pine boles in the fall at Schoolcraft State Park

Once you've felt it, you never forget it. It seeps into your soul, the North Woods, one of the most poetic spots on earth. It weaves a spell compounded of silence and beauty. It invites intimacy, with its solitary waterways spangled with water lilies and bird-song arias lofted from secret green hideaways.

Reeds at sunrise near Chief Wooden Frogs Campground,
Lake Kabetogama, Voyageurs National Park

Sunrise on Gull Lake filtered through the smoke-laden air of a forest fire in the Boundary Waters Canoe Area Wilderness

It is a land of form and symmetry. Tall spires of balsam and the spreading crowns of white and red pines brush the sky. Sun-seeking cedars lean over the water along the shore. In the forest, massive boulders brood in regal timelessness. Lean against one of these ancient monarchs and feel the evanescence of the mayfly. Run your fingertips through the boulder's mini-garden of moss, reindeer lichen, twinflower, and polypody fern. Find the bright yellow trailing root of the goldthread and follow . . . somehow inward.

Every lake has its own personality, a combination of size, topography, depth, and water color, the chance distribution of islands. Other factors are at work as well, even the type of rock most prevalent, from the bright pinks and whites of granite shorelines, laced with the fiery intrusions of rose quartz, to the dark, somber hues of smooth basalt. And there are the intangibles the traveler supplies him or herself, memories of past experiences on a lake or others like it, one's own definition of beauty, a mental image of perfection . . .

The canoe country inspires calm and introspection. Finding oneself under the impression of harmony and grace, and in the context of silence, a person begins to inquire, "What about me? Where is my symmetry, my harmony? How do I fit in?"

And the lakes . . . the lakes almost seem as if they are there to mirror the questions, to reflect the asker back upon him or herself and the imponderables of life, even as they reflect the trees, the clouds, the stars, and the moon at night.

Sunrise through forest fire smoke-laden air and red pine,
Gull Lake, Boundary Waters Canoe Area Wilderness

Rapids on the Kawishiwi River in the Superior National Forest

Rock outcropping and northern white cedar in fall, Boundary Waters Canoe Area Wilderness

Labrador tea growing in a black spruce bog, Superior National Forest

Labrador tea. It grows in low, wet places. In bogs and deep woods. Used by the colonists for a time after they dumped all the real stuff into Boston harbor. Is it good? As a gourmet beverage, probably not. But something about the lovely places where it's found, about gathering it yourself, leaf by leaf, about brewing it over an open fire under the stars, seems to make it . . . Well, it's still not very good.

Hoarfrost on spruce after a March ice storm, Superior National Forest

The universe is wild, game flavored as a hawk's wing.
Nature is miracle all.
—William James

Quaking aspen and blue sky in fall, St. Croix State Park

There are two ways to smell the astonishing sweetness of a fragrant white water lily. One way is to paddle your canoe up as close as possible. Then, taking care not to tip over, lean . . . way out . . . until your nose is only an inch or two from the blossom. Ahhh. . . . This takes some doing. The other way is, of course, to just fall out of the canoe. Either way works. Either is worth the trouble.

White water lilies on Big Rice Lake in late summer, Chippewa National Forest

Some days end with violent skies and windswept shores, lusty evenings of racing combers tipped with flame. But there are also those rare evenings when the world is quiet as a prayer, the canoe pushing its breast against reflecting waters, sky the iridescent hollow of a carnival glass bowl. Hushed shorelines reverberate with the last spiraling song of a thrush, the soft violin notes of a white-throated sparrow.

There is witchery in such an hour. You may have spent the day with a restless heart, an aching neck, a worried head. But you arise from such a scene transformed, and wander off to the bedroll to sleep the sleep of the just, the free of conscience, the good and the pure . . .

Sunset colors painted across Saganaga Lake,
Boundary Waters Canoe Area Wilderness

White pines in summer on a small island in Lake Kabetogama, Voyageurs National Park

"Quiet," whispers a voice from somewhere deep within. "Be still and listen to the gospel according to rocks, the gospel according to trees."

Red pine forest against the summer sky, Boundary Waters Canoe Area Wilderness

Stressed red pine on a rock outcropping, Boundary Waters Canoe Area Wilderness

Angles. The North Country is full of them— strong, clean angles. Perhaps that is why pen-and-ink artists have always loved it so and captured its essence so beautifully. The angle of a windswept pine against the sky, a dead limb. An overhanging cliff sheared off in clean breaks. The horizon lines of water, shores and sky, the rocky point reaching out from shore. And every angle an arrow pointing unerringly to the same ultimate target. You.

Summer sunrise on Eagle Nest Lake No. 4, near Ely

Right: Tracks across Rainy Lake at sunrise, Voyageurs National Park

Dawn. Mid-January. A remote and tiny island amidst the sprawl of Rainy Lake. The white pine mainsails look as if they still held last summer's wind. But there is no sound of wavelets chuckling on the shore, no song sparrow sings from last year's nest in the alders.

Yet here is the North as it has always been— defined by winter more than summer. The cold, the silence, the long, empty vistas, the feeling of reaching a place that is still somewhere "back of beyond" . . .

Windswept island in winter, Rainy Lake,
Voyageurs National Park

Cattails and red pine reflections in Deming Lake, Itasca State Park

"Still waters run deep." Not always true. But they do *reflect* deeply—the broad sweep of sky, framed by silhouetted pines or stained with maples, the passing form of raven or osprey, the drifting of clouds. In such a place even the sounds of nature—the rattling of a kingfisher downshore or the scolding of a red squirrel from the pines, the warbling of a winter wren from the deep woods, the gentle gabbling of blackducks among the bulrushes—are not so much heard as they are felt, experienced as part of the enveloping fabric of stillness. Here all the world seems up-gathered and focused, to be reflected back in greater clarity to the observer, the listener.

Reflections of fall colors, Shumway Lake, Savanna Portage State Park

Perhaps that is why no fine garden, no place of meditation or retreat, is complete without a reflecting pool, some focal point of blue. Why the most natural response in such a place is to stop. Become still. And reflect.

Lily pads and reeds in late summer, Lake Namakan,
Voyageurs National Park

Early morning light, boulders, and reeds, Boundary Waters Canoe Area Wilderness

Morning arrives wearing robes of crimson or royal purple. The wind still sleeps, the lake rests silently under its quilt of fog. From vague outlines of forest begin to echo the first tentative strains of the morning doxology—white-throated sparrow, chickadee, hermit thrush, from far downlake, a loon. And from camp the smell of coffee, bacon, and the simple greeting, now tinged with meaning . . . "Good morning."

Sunrise silhouetting red pine and spruce on tiny island, Boundary Waters Canoe Area Wilderness

It snowed last night, sometime west of midnight, and this morning the world is new. Tall pines and young balsam firs alike are clothed in mantles of white, stones wear high hats of snow. Out on the lake the first cold hawk of a wind dives out of the north, beginning to sweep shoreline rocks and trees bare once more, but in the woods all is still. A jay cries once and breaks the silence, but the sound quickly dies away, muffled by the snow. The jay calls no more—startled, perhaps, by what he has done. And the silence returns.

Fresh January snow blanketing northern Minnesota forest

White birch and red pine in January, Itasca State Park

Snow-covered waterway and driftwood on island in Rainy Lake, Voyageurs National Park

Rocky shoreline of small island in summer, Voyageurs National Park

Exposed bedrock shoreline and small island in Lake Kabetogama, Voyageurs National Park

There, across the lake or down the shore, you spot it, a bare finger of white granite or black basalt extending into the lake from the wall of trees. It's what every canoeist dreams of—the open, bedrock campsite with a view of sunrise and sunset, swept clean of mosquitoes by the breeze off the lake.

Paddle close and other rocky features become apparent—an intruded vein of rose quartz perhaps, the lovely pink shade resulting from contact with subterranean iron seepage; or a collection of sparkling slabs—gneiss or schist—arranged by some earlier camper into a fine stone fireplace. Just downshore from the point the shoreline warps and folds in tortured metamorphic layers bent by forces hard to imagine amid the present-day setting of lapping wavelets and silent cedars.

As much as woods and waters, the North Country of Minnesota is a land of rock. It includes the exposed southern edge of the Canadian Shield extending all the way to Hudson Bay; outcrops of meta-volcanic greenstones, at about 3.3 billion years the oldest rock in the canoe country; veins of quartz with enough sprinkling of gold to spark the Vermilion and Rainy Lake gold rushes of the late

Fall along the Laurentian Continental Divide near Virginia

1800s; and, in the search for gold, the discovery of vast deposits of iron ore, precipitated in shallow seas some two billion years ago.

The geologic history of the North Country is a collection of stories written in a tablet of stone, the last entries inscribed by the great glacial ice sheets that wrote in terms of carved-out lake beds and worn-down mountains, ten-ton boulders left where they don't belong, and deep scratches—striations—carved into the relentlessly exposed bedrock.

There's something humbling about scratching thoughts on a paper tablet while sitting on an outcrop the glaciers wrote on before leaving—for good?—some 10,000 years ago.

Dragonfly nymph case on rock ledge, Rainy Lake, Voyageurs National Park

Last summer an inch-long, underwater nymph climbed out of the lake onto a lichen-covered cliff, clung tightly, and ceased to be what it had been. Instead, out of a tiny split in the back of the old exoskeleton emerged something shiny and new and impossible—an adult dragonfly. For half an hour it dried gauzy wings in a soft June breeze, then left the past behind and flew into the open horizon of the future.

Six months later the old exoskeleton remains, clinging tightly in a January wind. Clinging tightly to the past.

Pitcherplant and other bog plants on floating logs, Superior National Forest

The bog is an integral part of the North Woods, yet it is an entirely *other* world, where "normal" rules of behavior seem suspended or reversed. Plants that eat animals, for instance (pitcherplant and sundew, devouring insects for nourishment); "land" that floats on water and quakes underfoot.

A bog is a living landscape of sphagnum moss, heaths and sedges, leatherleaf, bog rosemary, cranberries, and orchids, all forming a thick, floating mat that even grows trees—the black spruce and tamarack.

Steeped in preservative humic acids, bogs can hold hidden treasures. Long-dead animals and plants, even ancient human ancestors (up to 8,000 years old) have been found in bogs and fens in a near stasis, preserved safe from decay.

But the real magic of bogs is in the other, less tangible things they support and preserve. Things like wildness. Remoteness. Mystery.

Maple leaves dusted with snow, Lake Superior highlands, Tettegouche State Park

The first light snow of late autumn falls like a benediction on a world littered with fallen leaves and needles, a world spent from the reckless extravagance of summer, the last fiery displays of autumn. Time now for summing up and acceptance, the hush of anticipation.

All the North Woods waits as if holding its breath, the only sound the barely audible rustling of snow crystals, whispering as they descend.

Tamarack in fall at the beginning of the mighty Mississippi River, Itasca State Park

Near the transition of North Woods to Heartland lies Lake Itasca, Henry Rowe Schoolcraft's "true head" or source of the Mississippi. Out of the north end of the lake the water trickles musically between stones rounded by glaciers, flowing water, and countless bare feet. Perhaps never before have so many traveled so far to dip their toes into so little.

But there is a magic about it. And if you come at just the right time, you might have the entire "Father of Waters" to yourself. An October morn, perhaps, water and sky a startling sapphire blue, tamaracks blazoned in autumn gold, and a tiny, clear-water stream beginning a 2,552-mile journey—beginning with a soft chuckle, laughing, perhaps, at the audacity of it all.

NORTH SHORE

Rugged shoreline of Lake Superior at sunrise from Shovel Point,
Tettegouche State Park

Bedrock shoreline of Lake Superior, Shovel Point, Tettegouche State Park

All the old poetic phrases come quickly to the tongue. Gitche Gumee. Shining Big Sea Water. The Inland Ocean. Lake Superior is a dream, a mythical siren whose call has long bewitched those who love wildness and clean, hard beauty. The "Blue Profound" is the largest lake on earth, but was once larger still. The shorelines of ancient Glacial Lake Duluth were more than five hundred feet above the current level of Lake Superior and the glacial lake covered a much greater area.

Summer sunrise skimming across bedrock shore of Lake Superior at Grand Marais

Yet exploring the lake's rugged shore or navigating its waters, one feels no sense of the lake's diminution. Superior is, in depth, breadth, beauty, and majesty, the unquestioned monarch of the Great Lakes, sovereign of all the waters of the North. And upon her northern coastline rests a crown of waterfalls and silvered streams, known simply as . . . the North Shore.

Here among the ecology of the North Woods is a spectacular anomaly, an ocean coast of jagged hills, stony beaches, sheer cliffs, and carpets of roadside lupines, all bordering an endless expanse of blue.

If one loves rocks, woods, and waters, there is no better place to love than the North Shore.

Gooseberry Falls in late summer, Gooseberry Falls State Park

Superior's moods are endless, and can change as quickly as a thought crosses the mind, as dramatically as a smile or frown transforms the face. She lashes her coast with northeasters whose fury is hard to comprehend. She lies blue and still with a calm so profound that it, too, defies comprehension. For, like any great personality, it is not comprehension she invites. It is, simply, wonder.

Lake Superior shoreline on sunny summer day,
Temperance River State Park

Left: Lake Superior waves pound bedrock boulder

Summer sunrise on the shore of Lake Superior at Grand Marais

Summer sunrise lights bedrock and pools along shore of Lake Superior at Grand Marais

"To see a world in a grain of sand, And heaven in a wildflower," wrote William Blake. Or perhaps in a miniature world of creeping snowberry, twinflower and wintergreen, fairy cap mushrooms, club moss, bunchberry and British soldier and, dropped from some other universe of cloud and bird and breeze, a white pine cone, an oak leaf.

Bunchberry plants, reindeer lichen, and mushrooms in fall, Boundary Waters Canoe Area Wilderness

British soldiers (red crest lichen) and white-pine cone, Minnesota Point, Duluth

Mushrooms and bunchberries in fall along the Superior Hiking Trail, Superior National Forest

The Witch Tree, sacred spot of Native Americans, overlooking Lake Superior at Grand Portage

This gnarled little cedar, hauntingly poised and balanced, is well-known by its name, the Witch Tree. But it has another, older name as well—Manido Geezhi-gans—Ojibwa for "Spirit Little Cedar Tree." And this name comes closer to the truth. For more than a name or a famous image, this 400-year-old tree is a living presence, the distilled essence, or spirit, of a place. From its exposed perch upon Hat Point, it has received the tobacco offerings of the Anishinabe, witnessed the passing of their bark canoes and those of the red-capped voyageurs heading for Grand Portage and points beyond, stood through the ending of the fur trade, the arrival of the machine age, and weathered a countless procession of winds and storms and blizzards and droughts. All the while clinging indomitably to a bare rock outcrop overlooking an infinite expanse of sky and water.

Clinging still today, the little tree symbolizes the harshness, the gaunt beauty, the *spirit*—of the North Shore.

Sculpted by storm, winds, waves, and bitter cold, another North Shore appears in winter. A looming, forbidding icescape gives silent testimony to the raw power of the lake. But austerity is balanced by artistry. Symmetry and form, shape and shadow all combine to present a masterpiece of cold, blue silence.

In such surroundings, summer seems but a dream, while another age seems close at hand—the age of the mastodon and woolly mammoth, the age of ice.

Above and Opposite: Ice shoved up on shore from pressure of Lake Superior wave action in late winter

The Superior highlands provide that rarest of opportunities in Minnesota—the chance to view the world from a mountaintop. From a hard anorthosite outcrop that has long resisted erosion, one can gain the perspective of the broad-winged hawk or the eagle. On such an overlook, with time to gaze upon a quilted horizon of golds and reds and emerald greens, the true meanings of wildness can be sensed, the impact of solitude understood.

Mixed hardwood forest of Lake Superior highlands in fall,
Superior National Forest

Above and Left: View of the Lake Superior highlands from
Oberg Mountain, Superior National Forest

71

Palisade Creek collects fall leaves, Tettegouche State Park

When you fall in love with a place, you begin to understand it, to know it more intimately—the way fallen leaves swirl in an eddy, or a certain root curls around a particular rock, the way the moon and stars follow their old footprints across the sky—the same, but somehow different than in any other place.

It might even be said that you can't know a place at all unless you love it first.

Mushrooms along Lake Superior Hiking Trail near Leveaux Mountain, Superior National Forest

Tree to stump to fungus to soil to tree . . . life to death to life. Where does one stop and another begin? When we truly enter the forest, we learn that such dividing lines are hard to find, dissolving into a mosaic of constantly shifting shapes and colors and forms, a continually living world in which death is simply a stage of life, beginning as much as ending.

Bedrock and mixed hardwood forest from Carlton Peak, Superior National Forest

Long ago the Thunderbird flew recklessly through these woods, chasing the mythical Anishinabe hero, Nanabozho. The bird's wingtips nicked the birch trees, leaving the white trunks marked with black, wing-shaped scars, visible yet today.

Birch trees in Superior National Forest

Historic Split Rock Lighthouse, Split Rock Lighthouse State Park

Built in 1909–1910, after the damage and loss of many ships to Superior's November gales, the Split Rock Lighthouse has stood so long and lone and proud that it seems an integral part of the landscape—no more out of place than the waves breaking on the shore or the gulls mewling over the water. It operated until 1969, piercing the gloom with a ten-second-interval beacon and a foghorn that could be heard five miles away. Now it stands as a part of the diabase and anorthosite cliff on which it was built, sentinel and symbol of a bygone era.

HEARTLAND

Sunrise colors the National Wild and Scenic St. Croix River

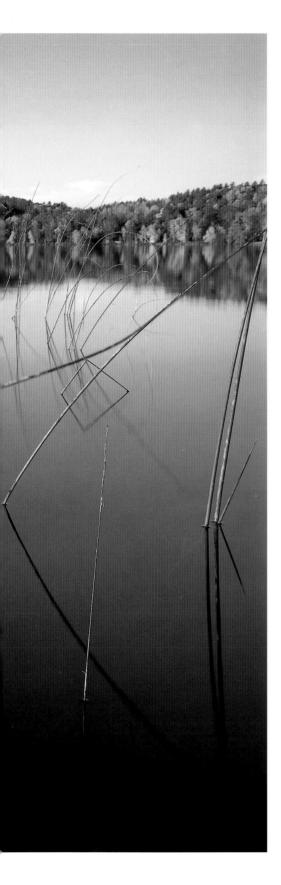

The Heartland is a varied, transitional area. It contains elements of the old Big Woods, North Woods, and Prairie, and is laced with rivers great and small. In large swaths it is studded with lakes, ponds, and wetlands cradled by sleeping hills—terminal and recessional moraine topography left by the Cary and Mankato substages of the final Wisconsin Glaciation. Bass and panfish, walleye and great northern pike swim these waters. Ruffed grouse and whitetailed deer inhabit the hills.

In other areas, the rolling terrain of drumlins, kettles, and eskers is juxtaposed with sandy plains, bogs and fens, and ancient lake beds, glacial features all. In fact, no area on Earth more clearly shows the record of Ice Age glaciers upon the land.

Today, the great ice sheets are gone, leaving footprints for an epitaph. Gone, too, are the primal silences of lakes that never echoed to the roar of an outboard or virgin prairies unacquainted with the plow. The once vast pineries of the Mississippi, Rum, Snake, and St. Croix valleys, the "golden triangle" forests of the logging era, have long since fallen to ax and saw, as has the contiguous Big Woods.

But Canada geese and goldeneyes still wing their way up the old river flyways, and hidden meadows still host the dance of the sandhill crane. The wolf is edging back from his stronghold in the north. Bloodroot and anemone still brighten the woods. And here and there a relic stand of old white pines yet commands the landscape. In the Heartland, for those who look and listen, glimpses of the old wild glory can still be found.

Reeds in Pillager Lake

Spring ferns along backwaters of National Wild and Scenic St. Croix River

Once in a great while you find it. Sometimes by accident. Sometimes after a long and difficult search. Then suddenly there it is—the scene that was in your mind's eye all along, the place you somehow visited long before you found it.

It's a secret place of emerald shadows and whispering silence, a place where Nature makes toy boats of worries and problems and sets them sailing on a quiet pool of dreams. . . .

Silhouetted maple at dawn along the shore of Lake Mille Lacs

. . . A place where time is suspended, eternity is a moment, and beauty is the
natural order of things. . . .

. . . And where all the other trails you have traveled come, for a short time at least, to rest.

The St. Croix River from William O'Brien State Park

A walk in the autumn woods is good for the soul. Perhaps there's a better way of putting that. More modest. One could simply say that a walk in the autumn woods is relaxing, or that it's good for the heart—all that walking and swinging of arms and cardiovascular stuff. One could say that it's good for the lungs—breathing in crisp, apple-cider air spiced with the scents of fallen leaves. One could say it's good for the eyes and ears and powers of alertness—squirrels rustling in leaves or leaping between trees, grouse exploding from aspen thickets, deer bounding out of buckbrush or prickly ash. Or one could say that it's good for your brain—getting away from schedules and ringing phones and whatnot.

And it is, of course. It's good for all these things. But it's probably more accurate just to say . . . a walk in the autumn woods is good for your soul.

Curtain Falls Trail, Interstate State Park

Left: Sugar maple in fall in Maplewood State Park

Sumac and maple in fall colors, Maplewood State Park

> *Everybody should own a tree this time of year.*
> *Or a valley full of trees, or a whole hillside. Not legally, in the*
> *formal way of "know all men . . ." and "heirs and assigns"*
> *written on a paper, but in the way one comes to own a tree by*
> *seeing it at the turn of the road . . . or in a park, and watching*
> *it day after day. . . . That way it is your tree whenever you*
> *choose to pass that way, and neither fence nor title can take it*
> *from you. And it will be yours as long as you remember.*
> *—Hal Borland*

Maples, sumac, and rolling hills in Maplewood State Park

... **A**nd if you have a favorite tree—an old bur oak maybe?—you might have a favorite time to go and see it. Sunset perhaps, or just after. Mood indigo sky. Moon tangled among black traceries of branches. Then faintly at first, growing louder, the wild barking of geese arrowing down the Mississippi. You keep watching—waiting to see if the arrow will hit the moon.

Majestic oak tree and January moon

A few warm breaths, a sigh or two, and Spring awakens. She waves a careless hand and suddenly the forest floor is strewn with whites and yellows, pinks and lavenders. Where there were only the damp ashes of last autumn's brilliant blaze, now crowds of flowers come out of nowhere to light up the earth. Trillium and bloodroot, marsh marigold, hepatica, dutchman's breeches, trout lily, spring beauty. . . . They arrive as if by magic to speak of spring and childhood and nameless little trickles of flowing water. To walk among them is to breathe the thick, pungent aromas of balm of gilead and moist humus, to listen for the silvery notes of migrating whitethroats.

Their time will not be long. Soon the upper canopy will leaf out once more and shields of shadow will deflect all but a few spears of sunlight. But now is the time of color. Now is the time of the shining woods. Now is the time of the wildflowers.

Field of marsh marigolds in full bloom in spring, Battle Creek Regional Park, St. Paul

Left: Forest floor carpeted by trillium in spring, central Minnesota

93

Do not needlessly destroy the flowers on the prairie or in the woods. If the flowers are plucked, there will be no flower babies; and if there be no flower babies, then in time there will be no people of the flower nations. And if the flower nations die out of the world, then the earth will be sad.
—Saying of the Omaha

Orange and Canada hawk weed, ox-eye daisy, and red clover in abandoned field near Esko

Season to season, the music of flowing water modulates, changing in mood and inflection. Early winter comes to central Minnesota and the songs are subdued, the harmonies more subtle. The stream still tumbles through the woods, falling over logs, swirling around boulders, dancing over riffles. But its voice is softer now. The water level is down, ice is beginning to form along the edges, dangling in crystal bells from dogwood twigs that brush the water. Listen on a quiet morning and you can hear the descant of a bell choir. Some night at twenty below, the music may stop altogether—or seem to. But listen close. There's a whispered melody under the ice—an echo of last year's summer, a promise of one to come.

Frost on branches and catkins along the Kettle River in Banning State Park

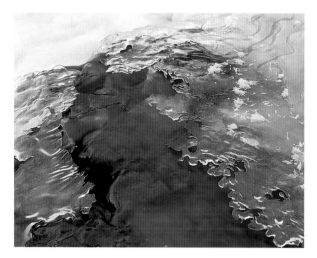

Melting river ice during spring thaw

Icicles on rock overhang along the Kettle River, Banning State Park

The Kettle River at dusk, Banning State Park

Waters have always been mysterious. Perhaps that is why they attract us so. It's an attraction compounded of many elements. For some it's the poetry of a dry fly laid perfectly on a black satin pool, or a spanking breeze on an open lake, turning the water to champagne. For others it's the slapping of wavelets on the shore, or the riffling of a woodland stream over logs and water-smoothed stones. All these are a part of the magic, but also there is simply mystery, the eternal mystery of waters.

Waters in their various moods and forms have existed as highways of commerce and barriers between worlds, the domain of monsters and the literal "ends of the earth," the reflectors of moon and

The lower Dalles of the St. Croix River, Interstate State Park

stars and of our own deepest dreams and thoughts. And waters are ever the settings for grand explorations—large and small, physical as well as spiritual—Columbus's Atlantic in this sense no different than Thoreau's Walden or Chuang Tsu's turtle pond, or the local swimming hole.

And today, in the age of fish finders and depth finders, sonar, radar, and kevlar, waters are still containers and revealers of secrets, still mysterious, still magnets to the human spirit. Just ask the old couple sitting by the lake shore, or the kid on the river bank with a cane pole in his hand. "What's in there? How deep is it? Where did it start? How far does it go? . . . Are they biting?"

In the transition from North Woods and North Shore to the central and eastern Heartland lies the astounding rocky gorge of the St. Louis River. Dropping hundreds of feet in its last few miles, the river and its Dalles are a remote and magnificent realm of water and stone, part of our heritage from the glaciers.

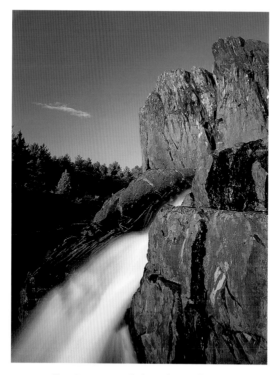

Evening summer light and waterfall in St. Louis River gorge, Jay Cooke State Park

Right: The St. Louis River tumbles over tilted slate bedrock in summer, Jay Cooke State Park

BLUFF COUNTRY

*Upper Mississippi River Wildlife and Fish Refuge
from Queen's Bluff, O. L. Kipp State Park*

Cottonwood tree in late fall

Why be out here? What's the purpose? What's the goal? Sometimes it's just the promise of new country, the feeling of looking forward to things you'll never forget, the pull of secret pathways and green arches in an unexplored woods, the view from a new overlook, a wider horizon. Sometimes it's the return to a favorite place as thick and sweet with memories as wild grape jelly. And sometimes it's the search to find a place where somehow, maybe for just a moment, you are in the still center of a spinning world, with the opportunity to simply "be."

View of Whitewater State Park in fall from Inspiration Point

Southeastern Minnesota is not a land of lakes, but it is still a land of waters—streams and rivers like the Root, the Cannon, the Whitewater, the Upper, Middle, and Lower Zumbro, and the by-now mighty Mississippi, gathering them in, all cutting and sewing this mature landscape, little affected by glaciers, into a silver-trimmed quilt of hills, valleys, canyons, woods, and wetlands. And when the sun rises through the mist, soft as the first dawn, one can almost imagine a morning half a billion years ago, rose-tinged mist shrouding a warm and shallow sea (the Ordovician) that stretched to what is now the Gulf of Mexico. It was that shallow ocean that lay down the layers of limestone through which today's stream beds and canyons are cut. Even then, a land of waters.

Summer sunrise over small pool, Whitewater Wildlife Management Area

Right: Whitewater River at spring dawn, Whitewater Wildlife Management Area

Spring tumbling from limestone formation, Richard J. Dorer Memorial Hardwood State Forest

Winter cress along Trout Run Creek in spring, Whitewater State Park

With its carved limestone topography, the Bluff Country is a rich tableau of cliffs, valleys, and overlooks. Underlying this visible landscape is a secret, interior landscape—a subterranean network of caves, fissures, sinkholes, and underground streams, cut into the ancient dolomite and limestone bedrock. It's an abundant country of rolling hardwood forests, clover and goldenrod and streambank wild grapes, white-tailed deer and wild turkey and brown trout. It's also the land where the Mississippi reaches full maturity and begins to turn her attentions ever more seriously toward other lands, other rivers, and other valleys—none more fair than this.

Upper Mississippi River Wildlife and Fish Refuge from O. L. Kipp State Park

View from the Mississippi River bluffs in fall

Sandstone bluffs against the sky, Mississippi River corridor

Red oak in winter, Afton State Park

Poets often speak of the many voices of the wind, but the wind is simply breath. It's the trees that give to the wind tongue and tone and language—they are the instruments through which it plays.

Each species of tree has its own voice, its own timbre. The pines moan, an ancient primordial sighing that seems to echo from the dawn of time. In the singing of boughs we can catch the first, faint hints of music and maybe wonder at its inspiration upon the dreamer of the first flute, the first lyre.

Dry red oak leaves in winter

No musicians the aspens and cottonwoods. They are the talking trees of woods and streambank, the slightest breeze enough to set them gossiping about the affairs of the day. Maple and basswood speak in calmer, more measured tones, waiting for something important to say.

And the red oaks, they wait for winter. Long after their deciduous brethren have dropped their leaves, bare branches whistling only in the strongest of winter gales, the oaks hold on, dry leaves speaking somberly of patience and perseverance, and other things that oaks must understand.

Winter sunrise through red oak branch

Mixed hardwood forest in late fall, Frontenac State Park

The dance of the seasons is performed in infinite steps and variations—the march of the woollybear caterpillar across the path, the timeless chronometry of color and falling leaves, the migration of geese and swallows and warblers, the abstract artistry of ice forming on a stream. All of it choreographed to the steady rhythms—the measured cadences of the land.

Fall leaves carpet Reno Bottoms, Upper Mississippi River National Wildlife and Fish Refuge

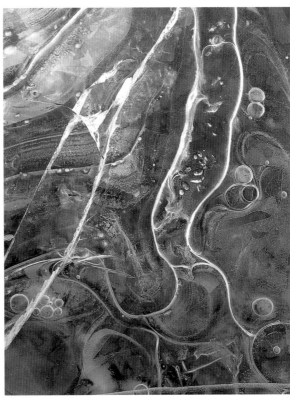

Ice patterns, Louisville Swamp, Minnesota Valley National Wildlife Refuge and Recreation Area near Shakopee

Left: Early December morning on the Cannon River near Red Wing

PRAIRIE

Lichen-covered Sioux quartzite and prickly pear cactus in July,
Blue Mounds State Park

Sioux quartzite boulders and summer prairie grasses, Pipestone National Monument

They traveled up to a thousand miles by foot to quarry the soft, red stone of the prairie—promised them by Wakan Tanka, Gitche Manitou, Maheo, Nih'ancan.

Here was a prime source of the ceremonial pipes used by the Dakota, the Oto, the Iowa, Sauk and Fox; the Kansa, Osage, and Arapaho; the Anishinabe and Cree; the Crow, the Shoshone, the Cheyenne; and by trade, as far as the peoples who lived near the great oceans.

But *here* was the sacred place, the place where myth and legend became real. Exposed amidst layers of hard quartzite was a mile-long bed of soft "pipestone," and here beneath azure skies and surrounded by an ocean of grass and wildflowers the stone was quarried. It would later become the bowl of a pipe, which would be used to conduct solemn ceremonies, to honor important occasions, and to offer supplication and thanksgiving to the Great Mystery.

Winnewassa Falls on Pipestone Creek in summer, Pipestone National Monument

Petroglyph rock carvings on quartzite ridge, Jeffers

If you are lucky, your journeys upon the earth may bring you to a place and a moment where time explodes, where the past is more real than the present, and where the old stories of the earth are laid before you—if only for a glimpse.

Such a moment may come at the bottom of the Grand Canyon or in the night fastness of a desert, beneath the stained-glass windows of a great cathedral or within the dim vaults and winding aisles of a redwood grove. Or it might come at early morning on an exposed quartzite ledge on the southwest Minnesota prairie.

The rose-tinged rock was deposited as a sandy beach by a sea now gone for half a billion years. In places you can still see the ripples. Worn into them and into all the exposed rocks are deep, parallel grooves—striations—left by the advancing mile-thick Des Moines lobe of the Wisconsin glaciation, some 12,000 to 14,000 years ago. And cut more deeply still, nearly 2,000 rock carvings of turtles, bear tracks, elk, bison, and stick-men warriors brandishing atlatls.

They were left, say anthropologists, during two distinct periods—the earliest depictions carved up to 5,000 years ago, the more recent produced by historic Indian peoples between 900 to 1750 A.D.

But in the first slanted rays of morning, the numbers blow away across the prairie, and in the breeze through the grass are echoes—of waves washing on a now-vanished shore, of the slow grinding of ice, of the *tap-tap-tap* of stone on stone, of humans communicating across the millennia.

Windblown prairie coneflowers in late summer, Crow-Hassan Park Reserve

Late-summer field of brown-eyed Susans, near Greenbush

On the prairie, vision drifts upon seas of flowers. It follows the waves of wind and rides them like a silent surf. Blazing star, brown-eyed Susan, coneflower, prairie smoke, undulating with the grasses, they lead the eye toward a far horizon and leave it there, resting against sky and space and the soft curve of the earth.

To walk a prairie is to understand walking in a new way. Here you are a creature of sky as much as earth, walking in a "world between," each small step a reminder of perspective, distance, balance.

Field of rough blazing star in late summer, Blazing Star Prairie, a state scientific and natural area in southwestern Minnesota

Prickly pear cactus blooms in mid-summer, Blue Mounds State Park

Cactus in Minnesota? In the land of lakes and loons and pines and . . . and on the southwest prairie, the startling yellow blossoms of prickly pear cactus. They lie scattered like gold doubloons, heedlessly dropped by cloud galleons sailing the sky.

Under storm clouds, prickly pear cactus blooms brighten the prairie, Blue Mounds State Park

Even on the prairie, Minnesota is about water. Here, too, the glaciers left their tracks — the prairie potholes, holding pintails and deer and leopard frogs; farther north, the remnants of glacial Lake Agassiz, once larger than Lake Superior, now drained toward Hudson Bay by the Red River of the north. And, here and there, even a waterfall, a place where in the Beginning Times, the Great Spirit's finger strayed a little longer, lovingly, leaving a touch of extra beauty.

Redwood Falls in spring, Alexander Ramsey City Park, Redwood Falls

Granite outcropping, marsh, and Minnesota River, Big Stone National Wildlife Refuge

Algae bloom on streambed in late summer, Red Lake River near Thief River Falls

I only went out for a walk, and finally concluded to
stay out until sundown; for going out, I found,
was really going in.
—John Muir

National Waterfowl Protection Area near Starbuck

Wild golden glow coneflower in summer along the Middle River, Old Mill State Park

Never does Nature say one thing and Wisdom another.
—Juvenal

Heath aster and smooth sumac in fall, Kasota Prairie, a Nature Conservancy preserve in southwestern Minnesota

When fall begins to stroll across the prairie, the sumac is among the first to feel its touch. It announces this occasion with a few startled stems of scarlet, which as the weeks go by, become beds of deepest crimson. And on some of the beds perhaps, a bouquet of heath aster, tossed there carelessly by departing summer.

Legend has it that Great Plains bison may once have been driven over these quartzite cliffs by early Stone Age hunters or, later, the Dakota. According to local folklore, great quantities of buffalo bones could be found at the base of the cliffs in the times of the earliest white settlers. No such evidence exists today, but the site is ideal for such a purpose, and similar to other kill sites across the Great Plains.

The red-tinged rock outcrop, up to one hundred feet high and one and a half miles long, came to be known to westward-moving settlers as the "Blue Mound." This seeming contradiction may simply have been due to its appearance in the haze of distance, or to the blue-gray lichens covering large portions of the rock face.

At the mound's southern end is a 1,250-foot-long line of stones, aligned east to west. It points perfectly to the rising and setting sun on spring and fall equinox. Who made it and why? Another mystery of the Blue Mounds.

Cliffs below a stormy summer sky, Blue Mounds State Park

Cliffs of Sioux quartzite rise from the prairie, Blue Mounds State Park

Today, big bluestem, prickly pear cactus, and hundreds of other native grasses and wildflowers are returning to this small bastion of prairie. The coyote's howl can be heard from atop the cliffs under a full moon. And a small herd of bison once more grazes the grass, but no longer are they driven over the cliffs. These stone ramparts now stand as a memorial to the age of the buffalo and the hunting cultures, and the once-vast prairie that supported them.

Prickly wild rose in abandoned summer field

To listen at evening as the meadowlark spins its last silver song, to lie awake at night and hang dreams from the stars while listening to the far-off timpani of night thunder, then to awaken to mist-shrouded pastels and soft greens of a prairie sunrise, all of this is to catch but a hint of the prairie as it once was—an endless sea of grass and dreams and opportunity, a barrier more fearsome than oceans or mountains, the defining heart of a continent.

Cobwebs and summer dawn mists in the prairie
of Blue Mounds State Park

EPILOGUE

The search will last as long as there are wild places and those who love them. It begins, this journey, with a simple thirst for beauty, a feeling for the land. It comes to rest on some forest trail or overlook, a hilltop or marsh or lakeshore, with a sudden sense of communion. Harmony. And a powerful feeling of responsibility . . . that this scene will be there for grandchildren yet unborn, and for those grandchildren's grandchildren.

The shining of pine needles in the sun, the sweep of a prairie hillside, the capering of waves along a lonely shore, the reverberating cadenza of a loon . . . and a love for the spirit of the land.

In Minnesota such things abide. May it always be so.

PHOTOGRAPHER'S NOTES

In landscape photography, the photographer records a moment of time, a tiny sliver of the ever-evolving world around us. As a result, an image or window is created that allows others to share a glimpse of what the photographer saw and felt.

For me, it is the pursuit, not the capture, of these "window-glimpses" that is most exciting. I know the entire experience can never be completely captured on film. There are times when my camera is simply put aside and just *being there* becomes the primary experience.

Yet it is in memory that such experiences live on and become a part of who we are; and photo-graphic images and nature writing have a way of tripping these memories. The sights, sounds, smells, tastes, even the physical feeling of an activity are again savored, and the joys of friendships recalled. Words and photographs can lift the spirit and set one among nature's delights once more. Doug Wood's writing does this for me. His words inspire me and expand the way I see the natural world. I thank Doug for the gift of his words.

It is our hope that this book will do the same for you—awakening old memories and rewarding you with new, yet timeless visions—visions of the beauty of Minnesota.

PHOTOGRAPHY LOCATION INDEX

Douglas Wood is the author of the celebrated children's book *Old Turtle*, currently in its twenty-third printing with over 490,000 copies sold. *Old Turtle* won the American Booksellers' Association ABBY Award, the International Reading Association Book of the Year Award, a Minnesota Book Award, and was chosen as the Midwest Publishers Best Children's Book for 1992. He is also the author of *Paddle Whispers*, and is the composer and performer of *EarthSongs* along with ten other albums.

As a wilderness guide, Doug has led scores of canoe trips from the Boundary Waters to the Northwest Territories. These trips — focusing on ecology, natural history, and personal growth — have included expeditions for the Smithsonian Institution, National Audubon Society, the Science Museum of Minnesota, and the Sigurd Olson Institute.

Greg Ryan's first loves were the woods and waters of Minnesota. After high school, he spent summers in Alaska, the Yukon, and Montana, cementing his decision to pursue a career where he could be close to the land.

He earned a degree in Forestry from the University of Minnesota and entered into a career in land surveying, pursuing photography in his spare time. After an extended trek through Nepal, Greg decided to pursue photography as a means to communicate his experiences, and in 1984 he began his career as a freelance photographer. His technical expertise and eye for composition have contributed to the success of his commercial assignment photography and the stock photography business he owns with Sally Beyer.

Greg's first book, *The Twin Cities, Naturally*, was written with Sally Beyer and was published by Voyageur Press in 1994.